SPIKED SCORPIONS & WALKING WHALES

Spiked Scorpions & Walking Whales

MODERN ANIMALS, ANCIENT ANIMALS, AND WATER

CLAIRE EAMER

annick press
toronto + new york + vancouver

Edited and copyedited by Geri Rowlatt
Photo research by Claire Eamer and Paula Ayer
Proofread by Paula Ayer
Cover and interior design by Irvin Cheung/iCheung Design
Cover illustration by Carl Buell
Cover photo by iStockphoto.com/John Bell

We acknowledge the support of the Canada Council for the Arts, the Ontario Arts Council, and the Government of Canada through the Book Publishing Industry Development Program (BPIDP) for our publishing activities.

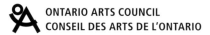

ONTARIO ARTS COUNCIL
CONSEIL DES ARTS DE L'ONTARIO

Cataloging in Publication
Eamer, Claire, 1947-
    Spiked scorpions and walking whales : modern animals, ancient animals, and water / by Claire Eamer.

Includes bibliographical references and index.
ISBN 978-1-55451-205-8 (pbk.).—ISBN 978-1-55451-206-5 (bound)

    1. Evolution (Biology)—Juvenile literature. 2. Phylogeny—Juvenile literature. 3. Animals—Juvenile literature. I. Title.

QH367.1.E238 2009   j591.3'8   C2009-901125-5

Printed and bound in China

Published in the U.S.A. by	**Distributed in Canada by**	**Distributed in the U.S.A. by**
Annick Press (U.S.) Ltd.	Firefly Books Ltd.	Firefly Books (U.S.) Inc.
	66 Leek Crescent	P.O. Box 1338
	Richmond Hill, ON	Ellicott Station
	L4B 1H1	Buffalo, NY 14205

Visit our website at **www.annickpress.com**

For Alan
Research assistant, sounding board, proofreader, and chef
With love

CONTENTS

> Busy as it looks, there's more life below the water than above it at this beach.

It came from the sea!

WHAT CAME FROM THE SEA? Everything. Everything alive, that is.

Stand on a sandy beach on a hot summer's day and what do you see? Life, everywhere you look.

People build castles in the sand, splash in the waves, and swim in the deeper water. Gulls swoop and scream overhead, shorebirds tiptoe along the water's edge, and insects buzz and flit through the grass above the beach.

It's hard to imagine that the invisible world beneath the water could be more full of life than the beach. But it is. A bucket of water from the top layer of the open ocean can contain as much life, in its way, as the most crowded beach—whether you measure that life by the number of creatures or by their amazing variety.

Long ago, in fact, life in the sea was the only kind of life on Earth.

And once upon a time, even longer ago, there was no sea on Earth and no life at all.

NICE WEATHER FOR DUCKS

TODAY, ALMOST THREE-QUARTERS OF EARTH'S SURFACE is covered by ocean. But the water wasn't always there. The oceans were created in the longest rainstorm ever.

When Earth was a newborn planet, more than 4.5 billion years ago, it had no water, no air, no life. It was a spinning ball of glowing, molten rock that boiled and roiled like the inside of a volcano.

A thick layer of water vapor collected around Earth, but the heat pouring off the planet's surface kept it from turning into liquid water. Some of the water vapor was created by chemical reactions within Earth itself. Some may have come from icy comets that collided with Earth.

For half a billion years or more, Earth slowly cooled. The rock on the surface turned solid, and then cracked and buckled and folded as hot rock beneath pushed and stretched it. The water vapor in the atmosphere cooled, too, and did what it does today. It turned into rain.

Earth looks blue from space because so much of it is covered by water.

Rain pelted down onto the cooling rocks year after year after year for thousands or, perhaps, millions of years. Water poured off the mountains and drained through the valleys. Trickles became streams, streams emptied into lakes, and lakes overflowed into great rivers. The water flowed to the lowest parts of Earth, gradually filling them up. By the time the rains slowed, at least three-quarters of the planet was covered with water. The oceans were born.

Life HAPPENS

SOMETIME IN THE NEXT FEW HUNDREDS OF MILLIONS OF YEARS, something strange happened in those oceans. Life appeared.

The earliest fossils of living things date from about 3.5 billion years ago. They're big mounds called stromatolites, made of layers of rocky material alternating with layers of tiny, single-celled life forms called bacteria. Bacteria are so small that 50,000 of them could live in a single drop of water. Bacteria may have been the largest living things on Earth for quite a long time, but they didn't leave much of a fossil record unless they massed together in a big mound. At some point, larger, single-celled organisms

Single-celled blue-green algae built these rocky mounds in Australia, just as they did hundreds of millions of years ago.

developed and evolved into creatures made up of many cells. But even after the creatures got bigger and more complex, they were still small and soft-bodied. So when they died, they were eaten by other creatures or they simply disintegrated.

When the main fossil record finally picked up again, though, it got really interesting.

ALiENS iN tHE ROCKS

ABOUT 585 MILLION YEARS AGO, the oceans were home to bizarre life forms that left fossil imprints in rocks as far apart as the dry hills of inland Australia and a layered sea cliff in southern Newfoundland on Canada's east coast.

The life forms that made those imprints look like nothing on Earth today. Or maybe looks are deceiving. It's hard for scientists to tell exactly what a living creature looked like and how it lived when all they have is the faint tracing of a long-vanished body that was flattened beneath millions of years of rock layers.

These fossils all appear to come from soft-bodied life forms with no sign of shells or hard body coverings. Some are shaped like spindles on a spinning wheel, some like feathers, some like disks, and some like plants. One of the larger fossils looks like a long, thin Christmas tree.

Whatever these organisms were, they belong to the past. After them came what is sometimes called the Cambrian explosion—a sudden burst of life that began in the oceans about 540 million years ago.

And that is where our story begins.

5

WORLD OF WATER

SOME OF THE ANIMAL FAMILIES in this book live in water their whole lives, just as their ancestors did. In fact, for some of them, life is much the same as it was hundreds of millions of years ago. Others have been transformed by time and changes on Earth.

Some are land creatures whose ancestors were water dwellers. Some are even water dwellers whose ancestors once lived on land.

Some live between the worlds of land and water. Is the platypus a land creature or a water creature? Or maybe for the platypus, it doesn't matter.

Ducks and geese have gone a step further. They've found a way to live at the place where land, water, and air meet. So what ties them to their ancient Australian relative, nicknamed the Demon Duck of Doom, a giant, flightless bird that lived a very different life?

The thing that ties together all of these animals is their link with water. And that's a link we all share. To find out how, read on!

6

It's a colorful world beneath the waves of the Red Sea.

HOW OLD IS OLD?

IT'S EASY TO SAY EARTH IS ABOUT 4.5 BILLION YEARS OLD. It's a lot harder to understand exactly how old that is.

Most of the time, we use much smaller numbers—10 pencils in a packet, 20 players in a game, or 100 pennies in a dollar. Even the larger numbers we use are small compared to the age of Earth. A big football stadium, the kind you see on television, might hold 30,000 people. It would take 150,000 stadiums that size to hold 4.5 billion people.

To make it a bit easier to understand what 4.5 billion years means, imagine squishing Earth's history into a single year. Each day of that imaginary year would cover about 12 million real years.

IN OUR IMAGINARY YEAR:

- Earth forms on the first day of January.

- Tiny, single-celled organisms first appear in late March.

- Bizarre soft-bodied creatures fill the oceans in mid-November.

- Two days later, the Cambrian animals appear—including segmented marine worms.

- About the third week of November, the ancient relatives of squids and octopuses show up.

- Plants begin covering the land at the end of November, while giant sea scorpions prowl the undersea world.

- Dinosaurs show up about three weeks into December.

- About the same time, platypus-like mammals settle into streams in the southern half of Earth.

- On December 27, an asteroid strikes Earth, bringing death to the dinosaurs and many other species.

- A few hours later, some ancient relatives of geese give up flying and settle down in Australia to become giant, flightless land birds.

- Less than a day after that, the ancestors of whales begin adapting to life in the water.

- And what about us? Modern humans arrive on the scene about 20 minutes before the midnight that ends our imaginary year of Earth's history.

An asteroid even bigger than the one that created this crater in Australia is probably what killed off the dinosaurs 65 million years ago.

IT CAME FROM THE SEA!

THE WORLD BENEATH THE WAVES

The deepest part of the ocean is Challenger Deep, at the south end of the Marianas Trench near Japan. It's almost 11 kilometers (nearly 7 miles) deep. If you plonked the world's highest mountain into it and stood on top, you'd still be 2 kilometers (1.25 miles) below the ocean's surface. And you wouldn't survive.

It would be black-dark and cold, with no air to breathe, and the pressure of all that water above would crush you. Humans can't live in the alien world beneath the waves, but for thousands of other species, it's home.

To land creatures like us, it looks like a very peculiar home.

For one thing, almost everything in the ocean can fly—in a sense. In the land world, we live at the bottom of an ocean of air. Only a few creatures can fly through the air, and even for them it's hard work. An ocean of water is different. Walking through water is hard work, but floating or swimming is easy because the water helps hold you up. Most water creatures float or swim well above the ocean bottom, flying through water, just as birds fly through air.

Another odd thing about the world beneath the waves is its layers. The deeper you go, the less light there is. The top layer of water, where there's enough sunlight to support plant life, is called the photic zone. But even in the clearest water, the photic zone is only about 100 meters (about 325 feet) deep. Beyond that, down to as much as a kilometer (just over half a mile), is the twilight zone, where a tiny amount of light reaches.

Past a kilometer, you enter the dark zone, where sunlight never reaches. The water is near freezing, whether the ocean is tropical or polar, and the pressure is enough to crush a golf ball. And yet there are animals that spend their whole lives in the dark zone.

A little marine worm swims in the darkness of the deep ocean, far beyond the reach of sunlight.

The tiny ancient worm *Burgessochaeta* emerges from its seafloor burrow.

WRIGGLING 'ROUND
THE WORLD

MORE THAN HALF A BILLION YEARS AGO, in the Cambrian geological period, the world was a very different place from today.

Earth spun so fast on its axis that a day was only about 21 hours long. The moon was closer and loomed much larger in the night sky. Its gravity pulled hard at the land and sea, creating huge tides that poured onto the land and eroded the rocky surface, then drained back into the sea, dragging sand and gravel with them.

The land was barren. Plants larger than algae wouldn't grow there for several more millions of years. But there was plenty of life in the sea—and plenty of sea for plants and animals to occupy.

The Cambrian was a warm period in Earth's climate history, with high sea levels. Shallow, salty oceans covered the land at the edges of the continents. About 505 million years ago, a small creature crawled across the bottom of one of those shallow seas. It was about half as long as a toothpick and looked like a miniature evergreen twig, with a narrow body and clumps of long bristles sticking straight out. It felt its way slowly forward, a couple of tentacles probing the muddy sea bottom ahead of it in search of things to eat.

Scientists named the little animal *Burgessochaeta* (BER-jess-oh-KEE-tah) after the place where its fossil remains were found—the Burgess Shale in Canada's Rocky Mountains. It is one of the earliest members of a group called the polychaetes (PAW-lee-keets), and its relatives—lots of its relatives—are still around in every part of Earth's oceans. They are so plentiful that if you scooped up a truckload of ocean bottom, about a third of the creatures in the sediment would be polychaetes.

BUNDLES OF BRISTLES

A small bearded fire worm shows off its body segments, typical of polychaetes.

POLYCHAETES ARE SEGMENTED WORMS, just like their land-based relatives, earthworms. Most of a polychaete's body is made up of a series of similar bits or segments, like beads on a string. Each segment has fleshy lobes sticking out from the sides, and clumps of bristles sticking out from those lobes. Slightly different segments make up the head and tail sections, sometimes with feeding structures or pieces that help anchor the worm to the sea bottom.

11

Burgessochaeta's trunk, the main part of its body, was made up of at least twenty-four segments. Each segment had four bundles of bristles, two on each side, with a dozen or more bristles in each bundle. It used the bristles like legs to creep across the sea bottom.

Some living polychaetes look a lot like *Burgessochaeta*. Others don't look like worms at all. They come in all sizes, from microscopic to huge, and in almost every shape and color you could imagine.

A few polychaetes are as thick as a fire hose and long enough to stretch across a classroom. Lug worms look a bit like bumpy earthworms. Palolo worms look like extra-long, round shoelaces. The feather duster worm looks like a feathery bouquet sticking out of a round handle. Christmas tree worms look like tiny, spiral-shaped spruce trees in unlikely colors, such as bright blue and yellow.

Almost all polychaetes live in the sea, but in very different parts of it. Some build their homes just below the high-tide mark, some float on the open ocean, and others spend their lives in the lightless depths.

They also behave very differently. Some live in tubes in beach sand and rarely come out. Some sit anchored to a rock in deep water and wave brightly colored feather-shaped tentacles to trap bits of food that drift by. Some cruise along just above the sea bottom, hunting creatures smaller than themselves. Some even live in the bones of dead whales or in the shells of hermit crabs.

HOUSECLEANERS IN THE BEACH

AS THE TIDE GOES OUT ON A SANDY SEASHORE, you'll often see small holes in the wet sand. After a few hours, you might find piles of sand near the holes. These piles look like twisted tubes, almost as if the sand has been forced through a drinking straw. And that's not far from the truth.

The holes are openings to the burrows of polychaetes. The sand piles are worm castings—basically, worm poop, the cleanest you may ever find. The worms eat sand as they burrow, and their digestive

Polychaetes, hidden away in burrows, leave mounds of processed sand on a Scottish beach between tides.

systems absorb the microorganisms and bits of plant and animal remains mixed in the sand. Then they force the clean sand out their back ends with enough pressure that it piles up on the beach surface.

Some of these beach dwellers are small, but others might be at least as long as a bread knife. Their burrows vary, too. Some dig deep into the sand, beyond the reach of a garden shovel. Others live in U-shaped burrows near the surface, pumping food-rich sand and water in one opening and pushing castings out the other. They wave their bristles to keep a current of water with food and fresh oxygen flowing through their burrows.

THE POLYCHAETES THAT LEAVE THEIR CASTINGS on the beach look fairly wormlike, but some of their relatives in the deeper water could be mistaken for blooming plants or particularly fancy party decorations. Take, for example, fan worms.

Fan worms are beautiful. They look like flowers growing up from the seafloor or from rocks in deep tide pools. Their petals can be white or blue or deep red or a combination of colors and shading. When you look closely at the petals, however, they're more like delicate feathers, arranged in circular or spiral patterns, sticking out of a hollow stalk.

The hollow stalk is actually a tube that the worm builds to protect itself, and the feathery petals are really elaborate tentacles that trap passing bits of food. The main body of the worm is tucked safely into the tube, which is permanently attached to the rock or sea bottom. If it senses danger, the worm can whip its beautiful fan back into the tube.

If it's not fast enough, and a passing fish gets a mouthful of worm fan, the missing bits grow back quickly.

14

A polychaete worm extends its tentacles into an elegant fan.

The fan does more than trap food. Cilia, little hairs on the fine branches of its feathery tentacles, wave to create currents that move bits of food toward the fan. The worm eats the smallest bits, usually algae or other microscopic organisms, and the cilia waft the larger bits back into the current or, sometimes, glue them to the worm's tube for support and camouflage.

This *Nereis* worm is so small that it had to be photographed through a microscope.

Hitching a Ride

SOME POLYCHAETES DON'T WAIT FOR FOOD to come to them. The little worm called *Nereis fucata* hitches a ride in the shell of a hermit crab.

Hermit crabs don't grow their own shells. Instead, they adopt the abandoned shells of other creatures. The worm makes its home in the upper part of the adopted shell, where the crab's soft body doesn't reach. Pulses from its little bristle-covered body keep water flowing through the shell to provide it with oxygen. When the crab is feeding, the worm creeps down lower in the shell and snatches bits of the crab's food, sometimes right out of its mouth. Then it retreats back into the safe upper reaches of the shell. The crab doesn't even seem to notice.

Young *Nereis* worms spend a while as free-floating larvae, then settle down and build muddy tubes in the ocean bottom where they wait for a hermit crab to come along. They apparently know a hermit crab is nearby from the vibrations its shell makes as it bumps along the seafloor. When a crab comes within reach, the young worm leaves its tube and scoots into the passing shell for a lifelong ride in its own private lunch wagon.

15

ALieNS ON EartH

NOT TOO LONG AGO, most scientists thought there was very little life in the strange world of the deep ocean. It's cold and utterly dark, and the pressure of the water is immense. At the deepest point, the pressure is more than a thousand times the pressure at the water's surface—strong enough to crush a normal submarine as if it were a pop can.

And even if animals could live in such conditions, what would they eat? The only food available would be fragments of organic matter drifting down from the sunlit zone far above, and that wouldn't be enough to support life.

Then, in 1977, a crew of geologists used a specialized underwater vehicle to explore a ridge more than 2 kilometers (1.25 miles) below the surface of the Pacific Ocean. They found hydrothermal vents, places where superheated water is forced to the surface by geological action deep in Earth. The water is full of dissolved minerals and hot enough to melt lead. Normally, water that hot would turn into steam, but the high pressure keeps it liquid. So instead, it boils out of the rock and deposits its minerals, building a kind of underwater smokestack.

The geologists were amazed to find the stacks covered with life. Clinging to the hot rock

Some hydrothermal vents, like this one, are called black smokers because of the color of the mineral-laden water pouring out of them.

and bathed in scalding, poisonous water were giant tube worms, some of them as tall as a man and as thick as his arm. Their tubes were white, and the frilly structures that came out of the tops of the tubes were blood-red. Thick beds of mussels and clams covered the base of each stack, hundreds of white crabs poked between the shells in search of food, and pink fish fed on swarms of little shrimplike animals.

The biggest surprise came when biologists examined these tube worms. They turned out to be among the weirdest of all polychaetes. They have no mouths, no guts, and no anuses. They don't eat, as we understand it. Instead, they're deep-sea farmers. Inside their bodies are colonies of bacteria. The frilly red gills at the top of the tube collect oxygen and sulfides from the hot water and carry them to the bacteria. The bacteria flourish, and the worm digests them.

For the first time, scientists saw life that didn't rely on the sun for energy. Instead, these creatures lived off the energy contained in the minerals pouring out of the hot vent.

Since then, hot vents have been found in the Atlantic, Pacific, and Indian oceans. All are populated by strange new creatures. Researchers have also discovered cold seeps, places where cold mineral-rich water seeps out of the seabed. Cold seeps also support colonies of animals, including slow-growing polychaetes that can live for decades or even centuries.

More than thirty years after that first colony of giant tube worms was discovered, one new species of vent creature is being identified every week or two. Many of them are our ancient friends, the polychaetes.

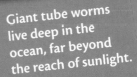

Giant tube worms live deep in the ocean, far beyond the reach of sunlight.

POLYCHAETE FAMILY TIES

THE ORIGIN OF THE POLYCHAETES is lost in time—a lot of time. It's possible that they had already been around for tens of millions of years by the time of *Burgessochaeta,* but it's hard to know for sure.

The problem is that polychaetes don't make good fossils. They usually get eaten first. Mostly, we find fossilized burrows and tiny jaws, the only hard bits of the worms' bodies. One of the few full-body polychaete fossils dates from more than 300 million years ago.

We do know that they're good at surviving. Polychaetes have lived through mass extinctions (like the one that killed off the dinosaurs), several ice ages, the movement of continents, and the opening and closing of oceans.

In fact, scientists have identified somewhere between 9,000 and 14,000 separate species of them in the world today and suspect there are many thousands more. Polychaetes all share, in some way, the segmented body plan with footlike bumps on the sides and bristles erupting from the bumps. It's still uncertain which other characteristics they all share and how they are related to other kinds of worms.

Christmas tree worms look more like decorations than trees.

FUN FacTS

In 1973, a researcher found 1,441 polychaetes, representing 103 different species, in a single chunk of coral weighing a couple of kilograms (about 5 pounds).

Polychaetes that live around cold hydrocarbon vents deep in the Gulf of Mexico take about 200 years to reach full size.

A 19th-century artist created this fanciful undersea world, filled with polychaetes.

Polychaete means "many bristles." In English, they are often called bristle worms.

Polychaete eyes have structures that link them to the eyes of both invertebrates and vertebrates, including humans.

Palolo worms break in two before they reproduce. Their front sections remain attached to the ocean bottom, while their back sections—thousands at a time—break off, float to the ocean surface in a great swarm, and release eggs.

The sea mouse is a hairy-looking polychaete that burrows in the sea bottom and stays out of sight, just like a mouse.

THE FLOATING GROCERY BASKET

Like many sea creatures, polychaetes reproduce by depositing clouds of eggs in the open ocean. The eggs hatch within a day or two, and tiny, delicate, almost transparent larvae drift up to the surface to join one of the world's great food resources, the plankton.

Plankton is a term for all living things that simply drift in the sea. Plantlike organisms in the plankton are called phytoplankton (FY-toh-plank-ton). Animals are called zooplankton (ZOH-oh-plank-ton).

Most zooplankton are tiny. Some are big. Jellyfish float in the ocean's currents, so they are plankton. The largest jellyfish species is the lion's mane jellyfish. The largest one recorded had a body big enough to fill a small bathroom and tentacles longer than two school buses.

The lion's mane jellyfish, the largest known jellyfish species, floats in the cold oceans near the north and south poles.

Each tiny diatom is protected by a delicate, glassy case, visible through a microscope.

Phytoplankton include big drifting patches of seaweed or giant kelp fronds, but most phytoplankton are microscopic, single-celled plants called diatoms. Each cell is protected by a delicate and beautiful glasslike shell. Some are shaped like wheels, some like lenses, some like tiny envelopes.

Diatoms are important as well as beautiful. The organisms that make up phytoplankton float near the ocean surface, where the sunlight is strong. Like plants on land, they convert carbon dioxide, sunlight, and other nutrients into organic material that feeds other organisms. In fact, they produce 90 percent of the organic material in the ocean. Plankton—phytoplankton and zooplankton together—feed, either directly or indirectly, almost every creature in the sea.

21

Cephalopods like *Cameroceras* ruled the oceans almost half a billion years ago.

THE EYES 3
Have It!

IN THE GREAT OCEANS OF 450 MILLION YEARS AGO, giant shell-fish cruised the seas, hunting for prey. One of the biggest and most fearsome of them looked like a rocket ship with tentacles.

Cameroceras (kam-er-oh-SEE-rass) had a straight, cone-shaped shell as long as a canoe. Grooved tentacles, arranged in a ring around its mouth, stuck out of the shell's wide end. Using a kind of jet-propulsion system, the animal moved backward through the water, shell first and tentacles trailing behind. It grabbed prey with its tentacles and shredded it into bite-sized chunks with its sharp beak.

This shelled giant belonged to one of the greatest marine animal families ever, the cephalopods (SEF-ah-loh-pawds). The earliest cephalopods show up in the fossil record about 50 million years before the time of *Cameroceras*, and its relatives still thrive in every sea today.

A HOUSE WITH MANY ROOMS

THE NAME *CAMEROCERAS,* MEANING "CHAMBERED HORN," comes from the animal's long, cone-shaped shell, which was divided inside into separate chambers. The animal itself lived in the largest, outermost chamber. As it grew, it built a new, larger chamber at the open end of the shell, and closed off the smaller chamber behind it with a thin wall called a septum.

The chambers were all connected to one another by a tube called a siphuncle (SY-fung-kl), which ran through a small hole in each septum. *Cameroceras* could use the siphuncle to move fluids and gases between its chambers. Modern cephalopods can make their shells more or less buoyant this way, and ancient cephalopods might have done the same thing.

23

A nautilus shell, cut in half, shows the chambers, the septa dividing them, and the remains of the siphuncle, the tube that links them.

No matter how well it floated, the shell must have made swimming difficult. *Cameroceras* swam by shooting a jet of water from a fleshy tube called a funnel. Although it could point the funnel in any direction, the long shell would have been hard to turn in the water. Probably it drifted in the current or swam slowly in the direction its shell pointed, just above the seabed, waiting for something edible to swim or crawl within reach.

For a smaller animal, being so clumsy would be dangerous. But *Cameroceras* was at least as big as any other animal in the sea, and its shell gave it all the protection it needed.

The chambered nautilus lives in deep water, out of sight, but nautilus shells sometimes wash up on beaches.

CONES, COILS, AND CORKSCREWS

CAMEROCERAS WAS AN ORTHOCONE (OR-THOH-COHN), part of a group of cephalopods with straight shells. Most orthocones were not big—some were as small as your little finger—but all of them had strong shells. They died out about 240 million years ago, but lots of their shells have survived as fossils, trapped in the rock of long-lost seabeds.

Other ancient cephalopods grew shells of different shapes. Some had simple, pointed shells that were straight like tiny tepees or curved like rhinoceros horns. Some had short, stout shells that curved in a loose spiral, like the horn of a mountain sheep. Others had thin, curved shells shaped almost like fish hooks.

Another large group, the ammonites, had shells that curled tightly back on themselves. Some curled around the same point so they looked like plates made of thick coils of pottery. Others formed spirals, like corkscrews. And some developed long spikes, perhaps to fend off predators.

For all their variety of shapes and sizes, cephalopod shells all have chambers separated by thin walls. A siphuncle links the chambers together. And the animal's living space is the last and largest chamber in the shell.

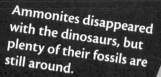

Ammonites disappeared with the dinosaurs, but plenty of their fossils are still around.

25

CAMEROCERAS LIVED WHEN EARTH WAS WARM and sea levels were the highest they've ever been. Life flourished and multiplied. But about 443 million years ago, temperatures dropped, conditions in the oceans changed, and many species disappeared—including the giant orthocones.

Although some cephalopod species became extinct, cephalopods themselves survived. Over hundreds of millions of years, they have experienced moving continents, volcanic eruptions, mass extinctions, changes to the climate and atmosphere, and ice ages—and they're still here.

When an asteroid crashed into Earth 65 million years ago, it not only caused the extinction of dinosaurs but also killed off the ammonites. Ammonites had been around for over 300 million years, and there were lots of them. Some were tiny, but others grew massive, coiled shells big enough to cover a dining-room table.

The ammonites lived in shallow water, and that may have been their downfall. The aftereffects of the asteroid impact killed off the shallow-water organisms the ammonites depended on for food. But deep in the oceans, beyond the reach of the catastrophe on Earth's surface, other kinds of cephalopods carried on with their lives. Gradually, they expanded and adapted to fill in the spaces left by the animals that died out.

26

SHELL GAMES

TWO MAJOR GROUPS OF CEPHALOPODS SURVIVE TODAY. One is a fairly small group made up of the nautiluses—deep-sea animals with coiled shells and dozens of tentacles. The animals in the other, much larger group have very small shells or no shells at all. This group includes octopuses, squids, and cuttlefish.

How can an eight-armed octopus with almost no shell be related to an animal with a heavy, coiled shell and dozens of short tentacles? Inside the nautilus's shell is a little animal that looks much like a small octopus or squid. It has a funnel-like structure, a circle of arms around a beaked mouth, and a mantle, the fleshy sac that contains its internal organs—all the basic cephalopod equipment.

Squids and cuttlefish have kept shells of a sort, but they carry them inside their bodies. The squid's shell is thin and pencil-like. The cuttlefish shell is a chalky internal plate that helps stiffen the mantle. When the plates of dead cuttlefish wash up on beaches, they're often sold as toys for pet birds under the name "cuttlebones."

A cuttlefish hovers over a reef.

MODERN CEPHALOPODS ARE FAMOUS FOR THEIR EYES.

Octopuses, squids, and cuttlefish all have camera eyes. That's the same kind of eye humans and other vertebrates have. As the name suggests, it works like the camera you use for taking photographs. There's a lens at the front, a dark chamber in the middle, and a kind of screen made of light sensors at the back. Light enters through the lens, which focuses a clear image on the screen at the back. In a camera, the image is recorded on film or in digital memory. In animals, the brain records and interprets the image.

Some cephalopod eyes are amazing. For example, the colossal squid, a deep-sea giant big enough to battle enormous whales, has the largest eyes in the animal world. One that was examined at a New

Eyes ON View

Zealand museum had eyes as wide across as a dinner plate, much larger than the eyes of the world's biggest animal, the blue whale.

Another oddity is a much smaller deep-sea creature sometimes called the cock-eyed squid. It has one small eye and one much larger eye, and it swims with its larger eye aimed toward the ocean's surface. The squid might be using the eye to spot prey outlined against the light far above, or to watch for upper-ocean predators like whales.

Baby cuttlefish live much closer to the surface and use their eyes even before they hatch. To test the babies' ability to see and learn, scientists raised cuttlefish eggs in an aquarium with crabs on the other side of a transparent divider. Cuttlefish normally hunt shrimp, but after the aquarium cuttlefish hatched, they went hunting crab as soon as they were big enough. It seems that baby cuttlefish sit in their translucent eggshells and watch the world outside, learning what's good to eat even before they're ready to eat it.

A squid keeps a wary eye on the photographer.

THE VAMPIRE

THE VAMPIRE SQUID, *VAMPYROTEUTHIS INFERNALIS*
(VAM-pee-roh-TEW-thiss in-FER-nah-liss), also has strange
eyes. But then, everything about it is strange. Its Latin name
means "vampire squid from hell," and it's the only survivor
of a very ancient family that falls somewhere between the
octopus and the squid.

This small deep-ocean cephalopod grows to about
the size of an American football. Its body is dark red
to black, and it has eight arms connected by skin
webbing. When its arms are extended, the webbing
looks batlike—probably why it's called the vampire
squid. It also has two long, thin tentacles it can tuck away
in pockets in the skin webbing. And it has two big, blue eyes,
so big that even a half-grown vampire squid has eyes about the
same size as those of a large dog.

Vampyroteuthis infernalis has webs of skin between its arms.

But perhaps the most astonishing thing about this squid is the
light show it can put on. It has large light-emitting organs behind
its two fins and smaller light-emitting organs on the tips of its arms.
When the squid is threatened, all its organs glow and pulse with a
bluish light. The animal waves its arms frantically so the lights are
in constant motion, and it squirts out a kind of mucus loaded with
fragments of light-emitting material. All its would-be attacker can
see is a jumble of little lights that might or might not be attached to
the animal it intended to eat.

29

Flecks of iridescence show in the body of this reef squid, feeding at night.

DESPITE THEIR SIZE, squids and octopuses live fairly short lives. Most squids, for example, live only one to three years and die after they reproduce.

In breeding season, male squids impress the females with fancy swimming and by changing their colors and, sometimes, putting on a light show. Then the males tuck packets of sperm into the mantle cavities of the females to fertilize their eggs. Once the eggs are deposited on the seafloor, the adult squids die. Or, at least, most squids die. In 2005, in the deep ocean off California, an underwater camera filmed five female squids carrying bundles of 2,000 to 3,000 eggs in their tentacles. Scientists discovered that the females of this species carry the eggs for several months, until they break away and hatch into baby squids.

The largest octopus of all, the giant Pacific octopus, lives only slightly longer than most squids—from three to five years. During that time, it does a lot of growing. The largest recorded member of the species had an arm span long enough to reach across a two-lane highway. As big as it is, the giant Pacific octopus is rarely seen. It lives in a rocky sea-bottom cave and eats shellfish, crabs, shrimp, and fish, caught with its long, sucker-lined arms. After the female lays her eggs, she tucks them safely into a crevice in the rocks and stays with them for up to seven months, until they hatch.

THE TIP OF THE ICEBERG

WE'RE JUST BEGINNING TO UNDERSTAND how little we know about cephalopods and how varied and surprising they are.

For example, researchers recently observed octopuses at several zoos and concluded that the animals actually have six arms and two legs, instead of eight arms. They use the two front pairs of tentacles as arms, to hunt, swim, and hold things, and use the third pair as backup arms. The back pair of tentacles acts as legs, to propel the animals across the sea bottom or to push off when they choose to swim.

Deep-sea vehicles have discovered several entirely new species of cephalopod in the past few years. One is the strange-looking *Magnapinna* (mag-nah-PIN-ah) squid, which hovers above the seafloor with its long, thin tentacles dangling from what look almost like elbow joints. Another is a chubby, pinkish octopus with short, curly arms. Named *Megaledone setebos* (meg-ah-LEH-leh-doh-nay SEH-teh-bohss), it might well be the living ancestor of many deep-sea octopus species.

As well as having the largest eyes in the animal world, the colossal squid is the largest living cephalopod. It lives deep in the ocean, and it's rarely seen and even more rarely caught. Not long ago, New Zealand scientists got a chance to study a female colossal squid that had been caught, accidentally, by a fishing boat. It was as long as a motor home. Scientists think that some specimens might be almost twice as long, but they're still looking for a squid that size.

Captive octopuses get in trouble when they're bored, so aquarium staff often give them toys to play with.

31

Megaleledone setebos is the closest living relative of the octopuses' common ancestor.

CEPHALOPOD FAMILY TIES

CEPHALOPODS ARE MOLLUSKS, part of the same group as clams, mussels, snails, and a lot of other animals. Most mollusks live in water and have shells of some sort. However, the group also includes garden slugs, which live on land, and several animals with tiny shells or no shells at all.

Of all the mollusks, cephalopods are among the biggest, the fastest, and probably the smartest. They all live in salt water. They all have a circle of arms or tentacles, numbering from eight to dozens, which connect directly to their heads and surround a hard beak. The rest of the body is the mantle that contains all the organs. They all suck water into the mantle to breathe, and shoot it out through a funnel to power their swimming.

At least half a billion years ago, the ancestor of all cephalopods, past and present, lived in the ancient seas of Earth. Some day, with a lot of luck, we might even find its fossil. Until then, we can only see its descendants. A lot of them!

So far we've found more than 7,500 different kinds of fossil cephalopods, and we know that's not even close to being all of them. Almost 800 living species have been identified, and more are discovered all the time as scientists explore remote parts of the oceans.

There are about 93,000 species of mollusks, including all the cephalopods—and this little land snail.

FUN Facts

When it's alarmed, the vampire squid flings its arms back over its head and body, effectively turning itself inside out.

A nautilus trained to connect a flash of light with food can remember the training for up to an hour. Then it forgets. But the memory returns 6 hours later and lasts up to 24 hours.

Many cephalopods have pigment cells in their skin. They can expand and contract these cells to change the color of their bodies as camouflage and to communicate with other members of their species.

The brain of the colossal squid weighs about as much as a mouse and surrounds the squid's esophagus. Its esophagus is only as wide as your finger, so the squid has to tear all its food into tiny pieces to swallow them through the hole in its brain.

When a *Spirula* is alive, its spiral shell—like these—is hidden inside its mantle.

The tiny *Spirula* (spy-ROO-lah) has a spiral shell with gas-filled chambers inside its mantle. This lets it bob in the water, tail up and arms down, waiting for food to pass within reach.

Apart from the beak, nothing in the bodies of shell-less cephalopods like the octopus is hard enough to become a fossil.

UP AND DOWN THE ELEVATOR

The greatest migration on Earth takes place in the ocean every night, all year round.

It's not the kind of migration you see in wildlife documentaries, with huge flocks of birds passing overhead or herds of caribou flowing across the land. This is a migration of many different kinds of creatures, some only a single cell and others among the biggest animals on Earth.

34

Every evening, as the light fades from the upper, sunlit regions of the ocean, the creatures of the sea's twilight zone travel toward the surface. Some travel only a short distance. The smallest creatures might move only the equivalent of three flights of stairs. Others travel much farther.

In 1983, researchers working in the southern Pacific Ocean near the island of Palau attached tiny radio transmitters to four nautiluses—the slow-swimming relatives of the squid. They discovered that the nautiluses traveled up and down the side of Palau's huge coral reef. Every night, the tagged animals rose up the side of the reef to a depth of about 150 meters (about 500 feet), almost half the height of the Eiffel Tower. There they spent the night feeding. At dawn, as light began to penetrate the upper layers of the sea, the nautiluses dove back down into the darkness of the deep ocean, nearly 460 meters (about 1500 feet) below the surface.

The chambered nautilus is part of the ocean's nightly migration up to shallower water.

Some marine animals travel even farther than the nautilus. The lanternfish, a deep-ocean dweller as long as a pencil, is dotted with light-emitting organs that glow in the dark. It spends its days in the sunless depths but swims up to feed every night, making a round-trip of 3.2 kilometers (2 miles).

So many animals migrate up and down in the ocean that there's four times as much life in the ocean's photic zone at night as during the day.

Light-emitting organs glow on the underside of a lanternfish.

The giant extinct sea scorpion *Jaekelopterus* is the largest member of its family ever found.

A TALE OF A STING

4

WHEN ANIMALS MADE THE GIANT STEP FROM WATER TO LAND, a lot of them left scorpionlike footprints behind. And some of the footprints have survived.

Not long ago, a set of ancient footprints turned up in some rocks in central Scotland. About 330 million years earlier, the rocks had been the muddy edge of a shallow lake or swamp. One day, a bulky, armored beast with lots of legs and a long, dragging body lumbered slowly across the mud, heading...somewhere.

We don't know the beginning or the end of its journey, but we do have a record of the middle—footprints and the groove cut into the mud by its abdomen. Before the muddy prints could be erased by wind or water, sand blew into them and protected them. Over millions of years, new layers of sand and rock pressed down on the sand and turned it into sandstone, preserving the prints until a scientist looking for fossils spotted them.

The scientist identified the prints. They belonged to *Hibbertopterus* (hib-ert-OP-tuh-russ), a giant sea scorpion the size of a large desk and a member of an ancient and remarkable family of extinct animals called the eurypterids (yoo-RIP-tuh-rids). Although *Hibbertopterus* spent most of its life in water, the Scottish footprints showed it might have been able to live, breathe, and walk on land, at least for short periods of time.

A GIANT WITH SPIKED CLAWS

EURYPTERIDS ARE COMMONLY CALLED SEA SCORPIONS, although most of them lived in fresh water or the slightly salty water at the mouths of rivers. They had a long and spectacular history, beginning at least 460 million years ago.

Not all of them were giants. In fact, most were no bigger than a lobster. But a few were large enough and fearsome enough to scare off a shark.

Biggest of all was *Jaekelopterus rhenaniae* (yeh-keh-LOP-tuh-russ reh-NAH-nee-ay), a sea scorpion that lived about 400 million years ago in what is now Germany. It was 2.5 meters (8 feet) long, from the front of its blunt head to the tip of its telson, the stiff, tail-like bit at the end of its abdomen. So if it were stood on its nose in a normal room, its telson would scrape the ceiling.

We don't actually have a complete fossil of this creature, just a claw. But what a claw! About one and a half times as long as a carpenter's hammer, it's a powerful, spiked weapon that could have grabbed, held, and shredded the primitive fish of the day or even other, smaller sea scorpions. Those claws, and its powerful jaws

equipped with fangs, meant this sea scorpion could eat just about anything it cared to.

Scientists calculated its size based on its claw and the measurements of other fossil sea scorpions. One huge claw was attached to each of the animal's two large front legs. Behind these front legs were four pairs of smaller legs that it might have used to walk on the bottom of the swamp and a final pair of legs adapted for swimming. Most of the sea scorpion's body was behind its legs—a wide, flattened abdomen that narrowed toward the tail, a bit like today's much smaller land scorpions.

We know quite a bit about sea scorpions' bodies because they were arthropods, animals whose bodies have a hard outer covering called an exoskeleton. Modern arthropods range from tiny insects to crabs and crayfish. An exoskeleton protects and supports the body, but it has a drawback. It doesn't expand as the animal grows. Instead, from time to time the animal has to shed its exoskeleton, emerging in a new and larger covering. Many of the discarded exoskeletons of sea scorpions survived as fossils, giving us a good idea of what the animals looked like.

A New World Opens

WHEN THEY FIRST APPEARED, at least 460 million years ago, eurypterids shared an ocean world with giant, cone-shaped cephalopods that roamed the sea's depths, and strange fish with armor and no jaws. The land was still empty of life, except for patches covered with a thin layer of algae or fungus. In the shallows where fresh water met salt water, the only thing a sea scorpion had to fear was another, larger sea scorpion.

Once fish developed jaws and teeth, sea scorpions were in trouble.

By the time sea scorpions disappeared, 200 million years later, many plants and animals were permanent land residents. And the animals that still lived in water had changed. Now sea scorpions had plenty to fear. Fish had developed jaws and teeth that could bite through a thin exoskeleton, and some of the new land animals were big enough to snack on sea scorpion.

Sea scorpions never became land animals, although, as the Scottish footprints showed, a few of them could at least visit the new world. Caught between worlds and at the mercy of new predators, they died out.

Around the time they were disappearing, a look-alike group of arthropods was completing its move to land. These were the ancestors of living scorpions. They once shared the shallow waters with the sea scorpions and may have been related to them.

Landing on a Strange Planet

ANIMALS HAD PLENTY OF REASONS to move to land. Some needed to escape their enemies. Some were looking for a safe place to lay their eggs and raise their young. Some scavenged food washed up on the beach. Some hunted other animals that had gone ashore. Some moved just because it was a new place to make a living.

However, if your species evolved in water, it's not an easy move to make. Think of a fish stranded on a beach. It can't breathe for more than a few minutes, and it can't do more than flop helplessly. But put it in water and it scoots away in a flash. To survive and succeed on land, animals had to make major changes to their bodies—and arthropods had what was needed to make those changes.

The yellow-banded flat rock scorpion prefers a dry climate, even though its ancestors came from the sea.

Their exoskeletons acted like space suits to support their bodies without the help of water and to keep their moist insides from drying out. They already had legs for crawling across the sea bottom, so it didn't take much to switch to crawling across land. Best of all, they had a breathing system that adapted fairly easily to extracting oxygen from air as well as from water. Some living arthropods, such as beach crabs, can still breathe in air or water.

Scorpions adjusted so well to life on land that they now live in a huge range of habitats, from underground caves to high mountains, from rain forests to desert dunes. We've identified well over a thousand species and there are lots more out there.

THE STING IN THE TAIL

IN SOME WAYS, scorpions still resemble sea scorpions. At the front of its body, the scorpion has two large, armlike limbs ending in powerful, pointed claws. Behind those are four pairs of walking limbs, and behind the limbs is a long, segmented abdomen. Where they are different is the shape of their abdomen—a living scorpion's abdomen is narrow and can curl up over its back.

At the end of the abdomen is the weapon for which the scorpion is famous: its stinger. The stinger is a bulb with a long, sharp spike on the end. Inside the bulb are two venom glands. The scorpion uses its claws to grab its prey—usually an insect, a small rodent, or another scorpion—then arches its abdomen forward over its back, stabs the stinger into the prey, and injects venom. The venom attacks the prey's nervous system, affecting different animals in different ways.

The bulb on the scorpion's tail contains venom that it can inject with the stinger on the tip of its tail.

Some scorpion venoms are strong enough to kill humans, and others are no worse than a bee sting. Large scorpions with powerful claws usually have milder venom than small scorpions with weak claws. The longest of all living scorpions is the flat rock scorpion from southern Africa. As long as a milk carton, it has large, bulky claws, a skinny tail, a small stinger, and mild venom. In contrast, the deathstalker, a desert scorpion, is less than half as long, with slender, fragile-looking claws and extremely powerful venom in its stinger.

Scorpion venom can be especially danger-ous to children or people with health prob-lems. In Mexico, scorpions sting more than 250,000 people every year and several hundred of them die, usually because they couldn't get medical treatment quickly enough. But scorpion venom might also save lives. Medical researchers are testing a new cancer-fighting drug made from a substance found in the venom of the deathstalker scorpion.

WEIRD AND WONDERFUL

SCORPIONS HAVE SOME STRANGE TALENTS.

For example, it's hard to sneak up on desert scorpions. They can sense even tiny vibrations in the sand through hairlike structures on their bodies, particularly on their legs. Dropping a single grain of sand near a scorpion is enough to warn it that you're there. The scorpion can even tell what direction the vibrations came from and whirl around to face the threat—or capture the meal, depending on what kind of creature set off the vibrations.

Scorpions glow in the dark. Well, not always. But if you go out at night in scorpion territory and shine an ultraviolet light at the ground, the scorpions will glow, usually a bright yellowy green or bright blue. The glow comes from a mixture of sugars and waxes that forms a waterproof surface on their exoskeletons. Scorpions can see ultraviolet light, but no one knows if they can see each other glowing. Whether it helps the scorpions or not, the glow makes life a lot easier for scorpion researchers trying to understand how the little animals behave.

Scorpions are good mothers. Scorpions reproduce by means of eggs, but the eggs develop and hatch inside the mother's body and she gives birth to live young. The babies look like miniature, pale-colored versions of the adult. The mother loads them on her back and carries them around from a few days to several weeks. During that time she feeds them and gives them water. Once they're strong enough to hunt, they leave their mother and strike out on their own.

This emperor scorpion mother will carry her babies on her back until they can fend for themselves.

SCORPION FAMILY TIES

MOST SCIENTISTS AGREE that sea scorpions are related to living scorpions, but they're not sure exactly how the family ties work. Sea scorpions might be the ancestors of living scorpions or some sort of cousins.

Part of the problem is that scorpions, sea scorpions, and all their potential relatives are so extremely old. They're some of the first large animals in the fossil record. After all that time, very little is left to tell us what they looked like, how they lived, and who their relations were. It's like trying to recreate a thousand-piece jigsaw puzzle when you have only a handful of pieces.

Based on the few jigsaw pieces we have, we know that sea scorpions and scorpions existed as separate groups for hundreds of millions of years. But scientists are still trying to figure out the exact relationship between the two groups.

So how do scorpions and sea scorpions fit into the animal world?

Both belong to a group of arthropods called chelicerates (keh-LISS-uh-rayts), named for the fanglike structures near the animals' mouths.

Scorpions are classed as arachnids, the group within the chelicerates that also contains spiders and all their relatives. But where scorpions fit within that group is still a puzzle, since they have some features that link them with spiders and some that link them with sea scorpions. It's going to take a lot more study—and maybe some new fossil finds—to sort out these family ties.

A spider shows off the fanglike structures that give chelicerates their name.

FUN FACTS

Some scorpions take eight years to become adults.

The world's smallest scorpion would barely stretch across your thumbnail.

Scorpions can range in size from as long as a man's boot to even smaller than this little fellow.

Scorpions can eat large amounts of food, storing the extra nutrients as fat in their bodies. Some can survive a year between meals.

In 1980, an Argentine paleontologist discovered what he thought was the largest spider ever, a 300-million-year-old giant with a body the size of a large dog. Twenty-five years later, a British paleontologist realized that it was actually a sea scorpion.

Baboons consider scorpions excellent snacks and skillfully remove the stinger before eating them.

One of the largest ancient scorpions lived about 415 million years ago and was as long as a skunk, tail included.

NEW TOOLS FOR OLD ANIMALS

Paleontologists used to spend their time painstakingly chipping fossils from the surrounding rock and puzzling over fragments of bone or shell left by some mysterious, long-vanished creature. Today, they also have some new, high-tech tools.

Not quite 60 years ago, we figured out that the blueprint for every animal and plant is laid out in its DNA, the common term for the genetic material in the cells of all living things. DNA is a long strand of coded information, almost like a super-long sentence that describes exactly what a living organism will be like. Even more recently, we've managed to map genomes—the whole sentence, word for word, that describes a species of plant or animal.

These tools can tell us whether animals are related and how closely they're related. In northern Canada, for example, scientists are analyzing the DNA in caribou droppings that were frozen in ice for thousands of years. They want to know if those caribou have living descendants and where they've moved to.

A paleontologist carefully chips rock away from the ancient bones of a dinosaur.

Scientists have determined that the little lizardlike tuatara from New Zealand is evolving much faster than most other animals.

We can get another kind of information by analyzing changes in DNA over time—much like tracking changes in the individual words in that super-long DNA sentence. The rate of change in the DNA words tells us how quickly an animal itself is changing or evolving.

The answer can be surprising. It certainly surprised scientists studying the tuatara (too-uh-TAHR-uh), a lizardlike reptile from New Zealand that looks almost exactly like its ancestors from the time of the dinosaurs. When the scientists looked at changes in the wording of the tuatara's DNA sentence, they found it is actually changing faster than any other vertebrate in the world, almost ten times as fast as the average animal.

Analyzing the speed and nature of change in an animal's DNA can tell us how modern animals are related to animals of the past and, sometimes, how long ago they evolved into new species. Paleontologists still rely heavily on fossils and rocks, but gleaming new lab equipment now plays an important role in unraveling the past.

Little *Steropodon galmani*, an ancient platypus, was one of the largest mammals alive in the age of the dinosaurs.

As Strange

As It Gets

5

EVENING ALONG THE BROKEN RIVER in eastern Australia can be a noisy time. As the light fades, birds settle in for the night, but not peacefully. Sulfur-crested cockatoos screech at each other from the branches of their roosting tree. A loud *whump-whump-whump* echoes from bank to bank as a brush turkey launches itself into clumsy flight.

The quietest place is the river itself, where a V-shaped ripple moves soundlessly toward the bank. Then, barely visible in the shadows, the sleek humps of a head and back break the surface, and the shallow hump of a plump, flattened tail appears. A little mud-brown animal, half the size of a house cat, lifts its head higher in the water and reveals—a bill shaped like a duck's! It's a platypus, one of Australia's most famous and most puzzling native animals.

A Flat-Footed Duck With Fur

THE PLATYPUS HAS ALWAYS BEEN A PUZZLE. It has dense brown fur like a beaver and a flattened tail that, unlike a beaver's tail, is covered with fur. It has webbed feet, but its feet are also equipped with strong digging claws. And strangest of all, it has a large bill shaped like a duck's, although it's soft and leathery, more like modified lips than a bird's bill.

In 1799, an English governor in Australia sent a dried platypus to London to be examined by scientists. The respected naturalist who first looked at it thought it might be a hoax—the skin of some mammal stitched to the bill of a duck. When he couldn't find any joins or seams, he decided it was a real—if very bizarre—animal, with a mix of features from birds, fish, and mammals.

He named the animal *Platypus anatinus*, which means "flat footed and ducklike." But since someone had already given the name "platypus" to a kind of beetle, the scientific name had to be changed. Today, the scientific name is *Ornithorhynchus anatinus* (OR-nith-oh-RIN-kuhs an-AH-tin-uhs), meaning "bird nosed and ducklike." For most people, though, the first name stuck, and the animal with the ducklike bill is still called a platypus.

The platypus spends most of its waking hours underwater.

After more specimens arrived in Europe, naturalists were prepared to believe that the platypus was a real animal, bill and all. They were even prepared to believe it was some kind of mammal, since they had proof that its young were fed on milk.

But they refused to believe another story that the colonists and Aboriginal people told about the platypus: it laid eggs. That, said the scientists, was just foolish. Mammals don't lay eggs. If eggs had been found in platypus nests, they must have been left by a bird. It wasn't until 1884, when a female platypus was shot just as she was about to lay an egg, that scientists finally changed their minds.

ONE OF A KIND?

FOR A LONG TIME, scientists thought there was nothing else like the platypus. Then they discovered another animal that laid eggs and shared some other platypus-like characteristics. It was the echidna (eh-KID-nah), a small, spiny insect eater that also lives in Australia. The two animals were grouped together in an order called monotremes (MAW-noh-treems), and they remained a mystery. No one could figure out exactly how they fit into the evolution of mammals. They seemed to be a tiny, lonely branch that had somehow survived or evolved in Australia, but nowhere else.

Although it doesn't look the part, this echidna is the platypus's closest living relative.

Things began to change in the 1970s, when paleontologists started to find and identify a treasury of new mammal fossils around the world, including in Australia. Since 1979, more than 200 new fossil mammals have been identified, some dating back to the days of the dinosaurs. Among them were relatives of the platypus. Suddenly, Australia's little monotremes weren't quite so alone.

A handful of fossil relatives of the platypus came from Australian locations. *Steropodon galmani* (stair-AW-poh-dawn GAL-man-ee) was probably the most important find. Discovered in 1985, it was an egg-laying mammal shaped like a plump platypus with a short tail. It lived in freshwater streams and lakes about 110 million years ago, during the age of the dinosaurs. Although it was only about as long as a small platypus, it was one of the biggest mammals in the world at that time.

The best-preserved fossil platypus is *Obdurodon dicksoni* (awb-DYU-roh-don DIK-suhn-ee), also known as the Riversleigh platypus. A complete skull with teeth was found at the Riversleigh fossil beds in northeastern Australia in the early 1990s. Today the place is hot and dry, but when the animal lived there, between 23 and 10 million years ago, it was a rain forest. The Riversleigh platypus was a bit larger than a living platypus and had an extremely long duck-bill snout with teeth. Adult platypuses today have horny pads in their mouths instead of teeth.

Branching Out

THE MOST STARTLING FOSSIL PLATYPUS FIND of the last few years didn't happen in Australia. In 1991, a few platypus teeth were found in South America, in the southern part of Argentina. The animal they came from probably looked like a very large Riversleigh platypus. It lived in South America about 62 million years ago, not long after the dinosaurs disappeared. But how did it get there?

Many, many millions of years ago, Australia was part of a great southern continent called Gondwana, which included Antarctica and South America. Gondwana slowly broke apart as the continents moved. However, at the time when the South American platypus lived, Australia was still linked to South America, probably by a series of islands that were part of Antarctica. It was still possible for animals to move back and forth between the two continents—and it appears that platypus ancestors did exactly that.

A few million years later, the continents were completely separate. The monotremes that had spread into South America died out, but those in Australia survived and continued to evolve. The only remaining platypus species, the animal that lives in Australia today, showed up about 1.6 million years ago—but now we know it's not as lonely as we once thought.

A Different Kind of Search

THE NEWFOUND FOSSILS TOLD US MORE ABOUT THE HISTORY of the platypus, but not about how it fits with other mammals. It's still strange. It lays eggs like a bird, it has skeletal features that resemble a reptile's, it feeds its young on milk like a mammal, and it even has venom like a snake.

A few years ago, a group of scientists decided to use new technology to solve an old puzzle. They mapped the complete genome of a platypus named Glennie. If you think of the genome as a long sentence describing exactly what a platypus is, this was a sentence with almost 16,000 words!

The genes of the platypus are just as surprising as the animal itself. When the researchers compared the platypus genome with the genomes of the mouse, dog, opossum, chicken, and human, they discovered that it shares most of its genes with mammals like us. But it also shares important genes and features with reptiles and birds.

For example, the platypus has genes for producing both egg yolk and milk. Birds, reptiles, and fish have egg-yolk genes, but not milk genes. Humans and other mammals have the milk genes, but not the egg-yolk genes.

Humans and other mammals have only two sex chromosomes, the bits of genetic material that determine whether an offspring will be male or female. Platypuses have different sex chromosomes

Some of the chromosomes in this bit of platypus genetic material have been dyed bright colors to make them easier to tell apart.

and more of them—ten altogether—and the chromosomes themselves are the kind that show up in birds, not mammals.

After looking at all the evidence, the researchers concluded that the platypus line separated from other mammals about 166 million years ago. That was not long, in evolutionary terms, after mammals evolved from a group of hairy reptiles, which is why the platypus still has some features that link it with reptiles. The two other great mammal groups—placental mammals, such as humans, and marsupials, such as kangaroos—divided 18 million years later.

Tasting the World

ONE OF THE DISCOVERIES THE RESEARCHERS MADE about the platypus's genetic nature helps explain how platypuses find their way around underwater.

Platypuses spend most of their waking time underwater, foraging for food at the bottom of streams and ponds. In many ways, they are as much water animals as land animals. They scoop up insects, crustaceans, and other small animals from the sediment of the stream bottom, stuff them in their cheek pouches, and return to the water's surface. There they grind up their catch between the horny plates in their mouths, swallow the meal, and dive almost immediately in search of another mouthful.

The platypus's bill has sensors that let it forage underwater without using its eyes.

When they dive, they close their eyes, their ears, and their nostrils. So how do they find their food? Part of the answer is in the thousands of pores on their leathery bills. The pores lead to touch sensors and to sensors that can detect mild electrical currents, created when water flows over obstacles. But another part of the answer is in their genes.

It turns out that the animals have a huge number of genes related to tasting and smelling things through their mouths—about a thousand of these genes, five times as many as most mammals. So platypuses may find their food by tasting the dissolved odors of animals underwater and tracking them down, even without the use of their other senses.

BOTH EGGS AND MILK

THE HARDEST THING FOR EARLY EUROPEAN SCIENTISTS to accept was the idea that platypuses lay eggs. They do.

Although we still have a lot to learn about platypus reproduction, we do know that the female platypus does all the parenting. She builds a nest deep in a stream bank and lines it with wet vegetation. There she lays from one to three eggs so small that two of them would fit on a 25-cent coin. The eggshells are soft and rubbery, not hard like bird eggs. She curls up around the eggs,

Platypus eggs are far smaller than these duck eggs and have soft shells. Tucked away in deep burrows, the eggs are rarely seen.

keeping them warm between her tail and her belly, and incubates them for about ten days.

When the tiny hatchlings emerge, they're blind, naked, and about as long as a jelly bean. They cling to their mother's belly, drinking the rich milk that seeps out of glands under her fur. After three or four months of living on milk, the babies are two-thirds the size of the mother, covered with fur, and ready to set out into the world.

HIDING IN PLAIN SIGHT

PLATYPUSES LIVE IN FRESHWATER STREAMS on the east and southeast sides of Australia, from the tropical north to the island of Tasmania in the south. That includes some of the more heavily populated parts of Australia. Nevertheless, many Australians have never seen one of these animal oddities except on a coin or a stamp.

Platypuses aren't easy to see. They're small and very secretive. They spend the daylight hours tucked away in their burrows. At dusk, they come out and spend the night hunting and feeding in the water, but they do it so quietly that most people don't notice them. They rarely travel on land because their legs aren't well designed for walking. At dawn, they crawl back into their burrows.

Platypuses are protected by law from hunting and trapping. It's not because Australian wildlife managers think they are in danger of disappearing. It's because platypuses are so good at hiding in plain sight that no one's quite sure how many of the little animals are out there.

Even though the platypus's entire genome has been mapped and we now have a good idea of where they came from, we still have a huge amount to learn about how platypuses live today.

Even in daylight, it's easy to overlook a platypus.

PLATYPUS FAMILY TIES

PLATYPUSES ARE MAMMALS, so they're related to all other mammals, including humans. However, the last animal that was an ancestor of both the platypus and humans lived about 166 million years ago, at a time when dinosaurs still ruled Earth.

Fossils show platypus-like ancestors going back at least 110 million years and living on two continents. Now there is only one living member of the platypus family, and it lives on only one continent, Australia.

The platypus has cousins, though. At the same time that more fossil platypuses were turning up, so were more living echidnas, the only other surviving mammal that lays eggs. The short-beaked echidna, which Europeans learned about a few centuries ago, lives in Australia and the surrounding islands. More recently, three rare species of long-beaked echidnas were found in Papua New Guinea—and there may be more, still undiscovered in that country's thick rain forests.

Baby echidnas hatch from eggs, just like baby platypuses.

FUN FACTS

The largest platypuses live in Tasmania.

The platypus stores fat in its tail, so a plump tail is the sign of a healthy platypus.

Female platypuses build long and complicated nesting burrows, usually with several linked tunnels. The tunnels are only as big around as a man's fist.

Adult male platypuses have spurs, on their hind legs, which can deliver a painful venom. The venom is strongest during the mating season.

A platypus swims through metal ripples on the Australian 20-cent coin.

Baby platypuses have teeth, but lose them as they become adults. Instead of teeth, they then have horny plates in their mouths to grind up their food.

Aboriginal Australians have several names for the platypus, including *Mallangong*, *Tambreet*, and *Boonaburra*. Early European colonists called it a water mole.

A large platypus is about half as long as an average beaver and about one-eighth of the beaver's weight.

Platypus milk is thicker than cow's milk and contains about sixty times as much iron.

EBB AND FLOW

The world of the sea and the world of the land are clearly different, but the border between them is anything but clear. It changes all the time.

Every day, the tide flows in and pours up the beach, covering the sand and rocks. It pushes its way up rivers, adding salt to their fresh water. It seeps into marshes and lagoons, bringing bits of seaweed, tiny animals, and a wealth of other nutrients to feed the lagoon and marsh creatures. And every day, it goes out again, pulling sediment and freshwater nutrients with it.

The area between the top of the high tide and the bottom of the low tide is called the intertidal zone. In some places, it's only a hand span across. In others, it's as wide across as a large field.

At high tide, these boats bob in the water, but when the tide goes out, they're stranded in the mud.

A lot of animals spend time in the intertidal zone—sometimes their whole lives. They have to be tough. Every day, they're covered with water for hours at a time, and every day they're exposed to the air, again for hours at a time. They need to breathe in both environments, avoid drying out in the air or drowning in the water, and protect themselves from predators. At the time when new worlds were opening up on land, the animals that scuttled around the intertidal zone were already equipped to survive on land.

The oceans also have a different, slower cycle of ebb and flow—of change. When the world is going through a warm period, the polar ice caps melt and sea level rises. During a cold period, the ice caps expand and sea level drops. The changes take place over millions of years, but they can still be fatal for animals adapted to a habitat that's disappearing. Or they can open up new habitats for animals that can change to fit them.

Large amounts of water are locked in glaciers like this one in Alaska. Some of that ice is melting today, causing world sea levels to rise.

WALKING BACK
to the OCEAN

6

ABOUT 49 MILLION YEARS AGO, A WARM, SALTY OCEAN called the Tethys (TETH-iss) Sea separated Europe and Asia from Africa and India, which was then an island.

On a sunny day long, long ago, a strange creature lurked in the shallows at the eastern end of the Tethys Sea. It looked a bit like a hairy crocodile, with a flattened body, long jaws studded with teeth, and a muscular tail. It crouched, mostly submerged, letting the warm water support the weight of its massive head. And it waited.

A flash among the reeds and a ripple in the water: a large fish had strayed into the sunlit shallows. The lurker watched and listened and waited until the fish came within range. Then it lunged through the water and clamped its toothy jaws on its prey.

Ambulocetus natans (am-byu-lo-SEE-tus NAH-tanz), the walking whale, had made a kill.

WHALES out of WATER

WE'VE KNOWN FOR A LONG TIME that whales are mammals. Like all mammals, they are warm-blooded, they give birth to live young, and they feed their offspring with milk.

Since mammals evolved on land, we also know that whales' ancestors were once land dwellers. However, it's a long way from an animal that prowls the shore on four legs to a giant whale that roams the deepest oceans. The walking whale was an important step along that path.

Ambulocetus natans actually means "swimming, walking whale," and the name tells its story. Its short, thick legs were strong enough to let it shuffle along on land, and its oversized, webbed feet equipped it for swimming. From nose to tail tip, it was almost twice as long as your bed and weighed as much as the largest tiger. And it was, indeed, a whale—one of a group of ancient, extinct whales.

The sea where the walking whale once lived no longer exists. The great plates that make up the surface of Earth shifted, and India crashed into Asia with a slow force that pinched off the sea and pushed the land upward to form the world's highest mountains. The shallows where the creature once lurked are now the high, dry Himalayan foothills of Pakistan.

And that's the place where, in 1992, scientists found an almost-complete fossil skeleton of *Ambulocetus,* locked nose down in rock that had once been seabed. They carefully chipped the rock away from the remains of the tail, the hind legs, the spine, and then the forelegs. Finally, they reached the skull—and realized they had discovered an important piece of the whale evolution puzzle. The four-legged skeleton had whale ear bones.

Past and Future in the Bones

THE TINY BONES INSIDE THE EARS OF WHALES and other members of their family, the cetaceans (seh-TAY-see-ans), have a peculiar, twisted shape that isn't found in any other group of mammals. It's part of the adaptations that let them hear in water. So when you find those ear bones, you know you have a whale.

Researchers had already found cetacean ear bones in the fossil remains of pakicetids (pak-ih-SEH-tids), animals that lived near the Tethys Sea a few million years before the walking whale. These whale

Unlikely as it seems, giraffes are descended from the same group of animals as whales.

ancestors—four-legged, hoofed animals shaped a bit like a cross between a wolf and a hyena—lived partly on land and likely spent a lot of time wading in shallow water on their thick, heavy legs.

Cetacean ear bones had also been found in fossils of animals that lived a few million years after the walking whale. These animals were completely adapted to the ocean, much like modern whales. But the walking-whale fossil was the first one that showed ancient whales in the process of adapting to life in water.

The specialized hand and foot bones of its skeleton linked it to another animal family— hoofed animals called artiodactyls (AR-tee-oh-DAK-tills). The fossil even had toes ending in hoofs that resembled thick, horny toenails. That confirmed what some scientists had suspected—whales are distantly related to modern artiodactyls, such as camels, pigs, cows, hippopotamuses, and giraffes.

WHALES TAKE THE PLUNGE

WE CAN ONLY GUESS why whale ancestors began moving back to the sea 55 million years ago. It was a warm, wet period in Earth's history, with lots of marshes, estuaries, and warm, shallow oceans. Perhaps the wetlands provided good hunting grounds for animals prepared to venture into the water.

It wasn't easy for whales to move back into the sea full-time. They had to make some adjustments.

First, they had to develop better bodies for swimming. The walking whale had already developed large, webbed feet. In later whales, the webbed feet of the front limbs became flippers and the legs themselves mostly disappeared into the whale's body. The back legs, which didn't help with swimming, gradually disappeared altogether.

In the meantime, their bodies were growing longer and more streamlined, better for moving through water. They developed wide, fin-shaped flukes on either side of their tails. Unlike fish and reptiles, which swim by moving their tails from side to side, whales move their tails and part of their bodies up and down, giving them an extremely powerful swimming stroke.

Second, they had to solve the problem of breathing air while living in water. Over millions of years, their nostrils moved from the end of the snout to the top of the head. This lets them inhale a huge gulp of air just by swimming briefly to the water's surface.

Third, they had to find a new way to stay warm. Hair and fur hold in heat on land but don't work well in water. For whales, the solution was to develop insulation inside the body: a thick layer of fat, called blubber, just under the skin. Once they had blubber, whales could live in any ocean, warm or cold.

Whales are such powerful swimmers that they can leap right out of the water, as this orca mother and calf are doing.

66

THE GREAT DIVIDE

SOMETIME BEFORE 23 MILLION YEARS AGO, whales split into two great tribes that survive to this day: baleen whales, also called mysticetes (MISS-tih-seets), and toothed whales, the odontocetes (oh-DON-toh-seets).

About thirteen species of living baleen whales have been identified, including most of the large whales. Instead of teeth, their mouths contain a forest of narrow plates, often fringed and made of a substance much like our fingernails. The whales use these plates, called baleen, as strainers. They gulp mouthfuls of seawater or sediment and use their huge tongues to push the water and fine sediment back out of their mouths. Any animals that happen to be in the water or sediment are trapped behind the baleen plates and swallowed.

A humpback whale scoops a mouthful of water and food, its baleen hanging from its upper jaw.

The other whale tribe, the toothed whales, includes more than seventy species—from the giant sperm whale to small whale cousins called dolphins and porpoises. They have kept their teeth, but the number and kind vary widely. The common dolphin has up to 250 teeth. A male narwhal usually has only one, but it's spectacular. It grows through the whale's upper lip, forming an ivory tusk as much as 2 meters (over 6 feet) long.

A bottlenose dolphin rises out of the water, showing its teeth.

The narwhal's tusk is just one of the mysteries of whales. Another mystery is how many kinds of whales survive today. Some are known only from a few carcasses or bones washed up on remote beaches.

What we do know is that whales are astonishing. They range in size from barely bigger than a human to the largest animal that has ever lived on Earth. They live in places as different as muddy rivers and the depths of polar oceans. Some sing long, complex songs and communicate across great distances with sound alone. Some migrate across almost half the globe.

Monster
of the Deep

THE MOST IMPRESSIVE RECORD HELD BY WHALES is biggest animal of all time. The blue whale is twice as big as the largest dinosaur that ever lived. An adult female blue whale can grow up to 33 meters (108 feet) long. If three whales that size were laid end to end, they would cover the length of a football field. The blue whale's tongue alone can weigh as much as an elephant.

Blue whales' mouths are filled with anywhere from 270 to 400 stiff strips of baleen, each one longer than a baseball bat. The whale uses the baleen to catch shrimplike creatures called krill, which are about the size of your finger. Blue whales live almost entirely on krill. Huge swarms of krill gather in the cold seas around Antarctica, and a blue whale will swim through a krill swarm with its great mouth open, gulping in both krill and ocean. Then it pushes the water back out with its tongue, trapping the krill among its baleen plates.

It's not surprising that it takes a lot of dinner to keep a blue whale going. What is surprising is that blue whales don't eat for half of the year. When they move to warm oceans to raise their calves, there's not much in the water for them to eat. So they fast for six months and then go back to the cold oceans to fill up on krill—about 3 million calories' worth a day. That's equal to about 6,000 fast-food hamburgers every day.

Krill, little shrimplike creatures, are the main food of the giant blue whale.

It seems odd that an animal as large as the blue whale would survive on such tiny creatures, but it makes sense. Swimming through a cloud of krill and straining them out of the water uses far less energy than hunting larger animals, and almost everything in a krill is food for a whale. You just have to be big enough to gulp huge amounts of water—and the blue whale is certainly big.

DiVING INtO DarKNESS

SPERM WHALES ARE ONLY ABOUT HALF AS LONG as blue whales, but that makes them the largest of all the toothed whales. And they're pretty amazing too.

Sperm whales have the largest brains in the animal world. The brain of an adult sperm whale weighs about seven times as much as a human brain. Does that mean they're smarter than we are? We don't know. We don't know how to communicate with them to find out how they use their brains. We don't even know what they might be thinking about.

We do know they're incredible divers. Sperm whales can dive at least a kilometer (almost two-thirds of a mile) below the surface and stay down for an hour. There are reports that underwater instruments have detected sperm whales at more than 2 kilometers (1.25 miles) down, and they may go even deeper.

When this sperm whale calf grows up, it will dive to depths that would kill a human.

At a kilometer down, the pressure of the water on the whale's body is one hundred times the pressure at the water's surface. Humans can't survive at that depth, and only a few specially designed, extra-strong undersea vehicles can go there. How do whales survive?

Whales store large amounts of oxygen in their blood and muscles so they don't have to rely on air in their lungs when they dive. As a whale goes deeper, the pressure of the water flattens its lungs and squeezes its blubber, pushing the oxygen-rich blood toward the vital organs where it's needed. This makes the whale less buoyant and it begins to sink. Then it glides the rest of the way down with very little effort.

But why go so deep? That's where the sperm whale finds its favorite food, squid. The stomachs of sperm whale killed by whalers often contained thousands of indigestible squid beaks. One large whale had almost 14,000 beaks in its stomach.

WE TEND TO THINK OF EARTH AS PIECES OF LAND separated by water. From a whale's point of view, however, it's a world of water interrupted by some inconvenient bits of land. They are lords of the sea—and that's three-quarters of the planet.

Whales can find their way across thousands of kilometers of ever-changing, ever-moving ocean. They can dive to the dark world of the ocean's depths and find their way by sound alone. They can swim and leap and play in the water with more power and grace than any Olympic athlete.

One thing they can't do, though, is defend themselves against humans who hunt them for meat, for blubber, and for baleen. Two hundred years ago, oil made from whale blubber lubricated machinery. It was also used for candles, lamp oil, cosmetics, explosives, and margarine. Baleen has been used for everything from ladies' corsets to buggy whips.

Even the giant blue whale was in danger of extinction. From the time it was first hunted, in 1864, until the hunt was banned a century later, about 350,000 blue whales were killed. Today most whale hunting is banned or limited, but many whale populations still haven't recovered.

Whalers almost killed off many whale species. This 1852 cartoon shows a sperm whale taking revenge.

CETACEAN FAMILY TIES

The early ancestors of whales had four legs and were no bigger than these wolves.

WHALES ORIGINATED IN ASIA, about 55 million years ago, as four-legged, hoofed animals, no bigger than wolves, prowling through shallow water along the shore of the Tethys Sea.

Within a few million years, their descendants had moved into the water. Special adaptations, such as webbed feet and specialized hearing, made life in the water easier for them.

They also adapted to salt water. Chemicals in the teeth of the earliest whale ancestors show that they lived and hunted near fresh water. The same tests on the walking whale show it spent time in both fresh and salt water.

By about 45 million years ago, whales spent their whole lives in the water and could no longer survive on land. The entire change took 10 million years at most, a very short time on the evolutionary calendar.

And then, maybe as much as 40 million years ago, whales split into two lines. All modern whales are either baleen whales or toothed whales.

FUN FacTs

Baby whales have special flaps on their tongues that prevent their mothers' milk from washing away in the ocean.

Male humpback whales sing long, complicated songs that change every year. The songs sung by Australian whales are completely different from those sung by North Atlantic humpbacks.

The porpoise gets its name from the Latin word for pig-fish, *Porcus pisces*.

Fin whales are the only animals that always have different color patterns on the left and right sides of their bodies. The right sides of their lower jaws and baleen plates are always white, and the left sides are always dark.

A baby blue whale drinks as much as 100 liters (about 26 gallons) of milk a day.

The oldest fossil baleen whale found so far lived 23 million years ago in the seas where Oregon now sits.

The deepest recorded dive by a mammal—2 kilometers, or 1.25 miles—was made by a male sperm whale in 1991.

SALT AND SWEET

If you've ever got a mouthful of seawater, you know salt water and fresh water aren't the same.

Seawater is salty, but simply adding table salt to fresh water won't give you seawater. There's a lot more in it than that. Water is very good at dissolving all kinds of things. It falls as rain, flows down rivers, and pours into the great basin of the sea, picking up lots of passengers along the way.

Sodium chloride, or table salt, is part of seawater, but so are plenty of other substances. Sulfate. Magnesium. Potassium. Calcium. Plus tiny amounts of almost every element found in Earth's crust or in the atmosphere above it. The amount of seawater that would fill a milk carton has two large spoonfuls of salts and elements dissolved in it.

74

Salt crystals cover the shore of the extremely salty Dead Sea.

Seabirds, such as this gull, have a special gland—usually above their eyes—to clean excess salt out of their blood.

We can't survive by drinking salt water. Salt dries out our cells, so our bodies get rid of extra salt in pee. To get rid of all the salt in seawater, we'd have to pee more than we drank and we'd die of dehydration.

Some animals have found a way around this problem: the salt gland. Reptiles such as sea turtles and crocodiles have them. So do ducks, geese, albatrosses, and other seabirds.

The salt gland starts working when the level of salt in the animal's blood cells gets too high. It sucks the extra salt out of the cells and excretes it from the body. So, animals with salt glands can survive drinking seawater for weeks or months at a time. If an animal has a salt gland, it's a sure sign that it lives on, in, or near the sea.

Bullockornis planei was one of the largest of the dromornithids.

THE DEMON DUCK of DOOM

7

SOME ANIMALS LIVE IN WATER, some on land, and some manage to live in both. Waterfowl—ducks, geese, and swans—have gone a step further: they've conquered the air as well.

Every spring in North America, millions of waterfowl follow the melting snow northward, flying for days or weeks, sometimes from one end of the continent to the other. Their goal is to reach traditional nesting grounds that might be as far north as the shores of the Arctic Ocean. There they can find everything they need—land for nesting sites and grazing, water for food and safety, and the air that lets them travel anywhere and everywhere.

Ducks, geese, and swans have mastered the art of living on the boundary where land, water, and air meet. But a few of their ancient relatives chose a different road.

IN 1830, SEVERAL MEN WERE EXPLORING CAVES in southeastern Australia. One man tied his rope to a chunk of rock in the side of a tunnel, but when he put his weight on the rope, the rock broke. He took a closer look and discovered it wasn't rock at all. It was the fossilized leg bone of a huge bird, bigger than any bird still alive.

The bone belonged to a dromornithid (drum-OR-nih-thid), one of Australia's extinct flightless giants. At one time, the huge birds lived all across Australia. The biggest was tall enough to stand on the ground beside a single-story house and pluck shingles off the roof. Others were only about as tall as an ostrich.

Aboriginal Australians already knew about the giant birds. At least 30,000 years ago, their ancestors probably saw living dromornithids in the open forests and grasslands that once covered much of the continent. Fossil remains of the huge, flightless birds have been found together with stone tools and other evidence of human activity.

BIG HEAD, LITTLE HEAD

SO FAR, RESEARCHERS HAVE GIVEN NAMES to eight different species of dromornithids. For some species, they have most of a skeleton. But skulls have been hard to find, and skulls have told us the most about dromornithids and their relatives.

Scientists once assumed they belonged to the same group as other large, flightless birds like the emu and ostrich. Those birds have long legs, big feet designed for walking, long necks, and small heads. Then,

Emus, like this mother and chicks, have large bodies but very small heads.

in 1998, two paleontologists pieced together a skull and beak of one of the larger dromornithids, *Bullockornis planei* (BULL-awk-OR-niss PLAYN-eye).

That skull changed everything. It wasn't a small skull with big eyes and a short beak, which would have placed *Bullockornis* with the emus and ostriches. Instead, it was a huge skull with a massive, arched beak that took up about two-thirds of its length.

It had features that linked its owner to living relatives—but not the relatives the researchers had expected. The giant bird belonged to the order Anseriformes (an-ser-uh-FORM-eez), which includes living ducks, geese, and swans. Although it was a flightless land dweller, its relatives have conquered land, water, and air.

GROUNDING a GOOSE

HOW DOES A RELATIVE OF A GOOSE end up as a giant, flightless ground bird?

It takes time. The earliest dromornithid bones are about 25 million years old, but other evidence suggests these birds might have been around for 50 million years or more. At some point, the birds' ancestors found they could survive very well without flying, and they gradually adapted to life on the ground. Their legs got longer, their wings got smaller, and their bodies grew and grew. The biggest of them all, *Dromornis stirtoni* (drum-ORN-iss STIR-ton-eye) or Stirton's thunder bird, lived about 8 million years ago. As heavy as a horse, it certainly couldn't fly.

From a human point of view, it's hard to understand how a bird could give up flying. Most of us would love to fly. And when you see a seagull soaring over the beach or a swallow performing rolls and dives in the air, it looks as if birds love it too.

Flying is an excellent way to escape predators and a good way to move from place to place in search of food. But flying has costs. Animals that fly have to fight against gravity, which uses a lot of energy. Developing wings and flight muscles also uses energy that could otherwise be used to lay eggs or grow faster.

Flying limits the size of birds. They have to stay relatively small and very light to fly. They have to get the nutrients

Most living Anseriformes, like this swan, exist on the boundaries of land, sea, and air.

79

out of food quickly and get rid of the stuff they can't use so it doesn't weigh them down. That's one of the reasons birds poop so much.

So, if there's plenty of food and not many predators, staying on the ground might be a good idea. And if there's plenty of food, getting bigger has advantages. Little animals like moles need to eat as much as half their own body weight of food each day, but big animals need to eat only a small fraction of their body weight. And really big animals, like dromornithids, get their first choice of food, just because of their size.

DeMON DUCK or GraZING GOOSe?

RESEARCHERS WERE AMAZED by the sheer size of the *Bullockornis* skull and by its massive beak. As a joke, one researcher nicknamed it the Demon Duck of Doom. That giant beak triggered an argument that's still going on in scientific circles.

The question is, what did *Bullockornis* and its giant relatives eat—plants, or other animals? It's not an easy argument to settle when the only evidence is old, broken bones. Figuring out what an animal looked like from a jumble of bones is hard enough, but deducing what it ate is harder still.

Scientists who think the bird was a meat eater—a demon duck—argue that its bill is too big and too well muscled for an animal that ate only plants. They see the powerful jaws and sharp slicing surfaces as evidence that it could eat meat as well.

Scientists who think it was more like a grazing goose argue that spongy bone and air cavities inside the great bill meant it was actually quite light. Most of the arch is a kind of crest that might have been used for display, like a peacock's tail.

Meat-eating birds, like this vulture, have strong, sharp bills designed to cut and tear flesh.

Canada geese eat almost anything that comes their way, including grass.

So, demon duck or grazing goose? We need more evidence—ideally, something like the fossilized remains of the stomach contents of one of the giant birds.

THE DOWN SIDE OF

BULLOCKORNIS PLANEI AND STIRTON'S THUNDER BIRD were the largest of the dromornithids, and they were spectacular creatures. *Bullockornis* lived about 10 to 12 million years ago and weighed as much as a medium-sized grizzly bear. Stirton's thunder bird lived a few million years later. It was an arm's length taller and weighed as much as a large polar bear.

Big animals make more efficient use of food, but they still need a lot of it. A single Stirton's thunder bird would probably eat the same amount as fifty Canada geese. A small flock or family group of the giants would need a large territory and plenty of food. That might have been what finally did them in.

Stirton's thunder bird became extinct between 8 and 5 million years ago. That was a time when its habitat was getting drier, and open woodlands and grasslands were replacing the denser forests that provided more food. At the same time, other Australian animals, such as kangaroos and wombats, were growing bigger. A lot of animals were competing for the food supply, and Stirton's thunder bird might simply have lost the competition.

Later dromornithids were smaller. The last of them was just two-thirds the height of Stirton's thunder bird and more lightly built. It appeared on the scene about 1.6 million years ago and disappeared about 30,000 years ago, at a time when many of Australia's giant animals went extinct.

FILLING the SKIES

DROMORNITHIDS MAY BE GONE, but their relatives still flourish. Today, more than 150 species of ducks, geese, swans, and a few other relatives live around the world, from Australia and New Zealand in the south all the way to the Arctic Ocean.

The Canada goose may be the best known of them all. It's so common in North America

82

that most people think its black head and white chin patch are the marks of a wild goose. Canada geese nest or winter in every Canadian province, in Northern Mexico, and in all of the United States except Hawaii.

Canada geese have even moved to other continents, with a little help from humans. At one time, they were kept in zoos in Britain and other parts of Europe, but some escaped and set up house in the local wetlands. They adapted so well that, today, Britain alone has more than 80,000 breeding pairs.

In North America, Canada geese number in the millions. They live in wetlands and coastal marshes, near lakes and rivers, and on prairie sloughs. And, as many of us know, they also live happily in city parks, golf courses, and farmers' fields.

Canada geese are a common sight in the skies of North America.

TRAVELS WITH tHE FAMiLY

WHEN YOU SEE A FLOCK OF CANADA GEESE passing overhead, you're looking at an extended family: mothers, fathers, the latest brood of offspring, and their aunts, uncles, and cousins. Goslings stay with their parents for a full year after they hatch, flying south with their parents for the winter and back north to their breeding grounds in the spring. Even after young geese set out on their own, the females return to the same nesting grounds—and often the same nests—their mothers used.

They live as a family on the nesting grounds and stay there all summer. The female sits on her batch of eggs for up to four weeks, leaving the nest each day for a quick snack and a drink. When the female takes her daily break, the male protects the nest. For the rest of the time, he stays some distance away but is always on guard. His job, if he spots danger, is to save the nest or lure the attacker away from it.

Soon after the goslings hatch, the whole family sets off for its chosen feeding ground, somewhere with plenty of nutritious food for the youngsters. The female usually leads the way, with the goslings trudging behind her, and the male acting as rearguard. The journey can take several days because, since the goslings can't fly until they're at least six weeks old, it's all on foot.

Canada geese stick together in family groups and take good care of their young.

LiViNG OFF the LaND

CANADA GEESE SHARE MORE WITH DROMORNITHIDS than you might think. True, the geese can fly and they spend a lot of time in or near water. But they also spend a great deal of time on land. Many other species of ducks, geese, and swans get most of their food from the water, but Canada geese feed on land.

In spring and summer, they prefer grass leaves, but they'll also eat leaves, stems, roots, seeds, and berries from other plants. In fall and winter, they look for grains and seeds. Human agriculture has made life easier for Canada geese by providing large fields littered with spilled grain, corn, or soybeans from the harvest. That's an energy-rich feast for a hungry goose in winter. Flocks of geese often spend several hours in the morning and evening feeding in farmers' fields. Between feeding sessions, they move to the water where it's easier to spot predators.

Canada geese have something else in common with dromornithids— the ability to adapt to new circumstances. They have adapted to new continents and to very different climates. Some gave up migrating when they found a year-round food supply. Others learned to live and raise their young in the middle of human communities.

The most extraordinary example of how geese can adapt might be the nene (NAY-nay) geese of Hawaii. Recent genetic analysis told us that nene geese are descended from a group of Canada geese that settled on the islands almost 900,000 years ago. Living on a few small, isolated islands for so long has left nene geese unable to fly long distances. They can still fly, but not very well, and they walk most of the time. They lost much of the webbing on their feet and developed long claws that make walking easier on Hawaii's lava rock.

Although clearly not the flightless giants of Australia, nene geese are an example of how Anseriformes can adapt to new surroundings and survive.

The reduced webbing on the feet of nene geese makes it easier for them to walk on the volcanic rocks of Hawaii.

Nene geese live in Hawaii. They can fly short distances but prefer to walk.

THE DEMON DUCK OF DOOM

DROMORNITHID FAMILY TIES

SCIENTISTS CONCLUDED ONLY A FEW YEARS AGO that dromornithids were members of the Anseriformes, the order that includes ducks, geese, and swans.

A swan stretches its neck underwater to reach tasty plants. The Canada goose watching it prefers to feed on land.

Dromornithid bodies were more heavily built than those of other flightless birds like emus and ostriches. Despite their size, both emus and ostriches are built for running, with long, slim legs, small heads, and a light build. The dromornithids had thick, strong legs and a heavy build. They could certainly walk efficiently but they wouldn't have run very fast.

Some dromornithids appear to have spaces in the skull for salt glands, a feature of birds that drink salty or brackish water at least part of the time. Salt glands are common among Anseriformes, as well as other seabirds.

Even though they share some features with living ducks, geese, and swans, dromornithids evolved in a different direction. That change might have begun more than 50 million years ago, but we don't know for sure. A fragment of leg bone found a few years ago in Antarctica might have belonged to a dromornithid and might tell us more about their origins.

There are a lot of "mights" in this story and there's plenty still to learn.

FUN FACTS

Canada geese use about thirteen different calls to communicate, including loud calls to greet other geese or warn of danger and softer clucks and murmurs when they are feeding. Goslings begin communicating with their parents while they're still in the egg.

Other giant birds of the past include the great elephant bird, the giant moa, and the terror bird. Of the dromornithids, only Stirton's thunder bird came close to their size.

Based on fossil shell fragments, scientists estimate that the egg of a Stirton's thunder bird weighed about 12 kilograms (26 pounds). That's the weight of the heaviest human baby on record.

The giant moa, which lived in New Zealand until less than 250 years ago, was taller than any dromornithid.

In some places in Australia, you can find piles of polished stones that once helped grind up the food in a dromornithid's gizzard. The ancient bird's body has disappeared, but the piles of stones remain.

Dromornithids had small, strong wings they could flap, even if they couldn't use them for flying.

In 1905, fifty Canada geese were brought to New Zealand for hunters. Now tens of thousands of their descendants live there.

87

POSTSCRIPT: LIFE WITHOUT WATER?

A postscript is a bit of information that comes after a book or a letter. This postscript is about information we don't have—at least, not yet.

Can you imagine what life might look like on a planet without water? Is it even possible?

Life on Earth came from the sea, and it still depends entirely on water. In fact, it's almost impossible to find a bit of water on Earth that doesn't have some sort of life in it.

All the animals in this story, and all living things on Earth, have a close connection to water. Even animals that live on land carry a surprising amount of water around as part of their bodies. People, for example, are about 65 percent water. Some jellyfish are up to 95 percent water. The first single-celled creatures that lived in the oceans were little more than tiny bags of water.

Jellyfish, like this one, can be up to 95 percent water.

Mars has frozen water, both in its polar ice caps and underground. Scientists are searching for signs that it once had water-based life, like Earth.

Water carries nutrients around our cells, around our bodies, and around the world. It ferries waste products away. It's vital to the chemical reactions that living things use to turn elements like oxygen and carbon into life processes.

We have sent spaceships all the way to Mars to look for traces of water in its parched soil, and it's headline news when we find them. It means life might be possible there, either for unknown Martian organisms or for earthling settlers sometime in the future.

Can life, in some form, exist without water? Both science fiction writers and scientists have speculated about life forms that depend on other materials—silicon, methane, ammonia, or something else. We haven't seen anything like that yet, but we've barely begun to look beyond our own planet.

And would we even recognize one of those life forms if we saw it? On our planet, Earth, water is so important that it's hard to see life any other way.

LIFE WITHOUT WATER

FURTHER READING

LIFE AND WATER

Census of Marine Life. **www.coml.org/** A website on marine life.

Hoffman, Jennifer. *Science 101: Ocean Science*. New York: HarperCollins Publishing, 2007. A beautifully illustrated introduction, in plain language, to the biology, physics, and chemistry of the ocean.

Tocci, Salvatore. *Marine Habitats: Life In Saltwater*. New York: Franklin Watts, 2005.

Woodward, John. *Oceans Atlas: An Amazing Aquatic Adventure*. New York: Dorling Kindersley, 2007.

POLYCHAETES AND THEIR WORLD

Beyond the Reef. **www.amonline.net.au/exhibitions/beyond** An online exhibit of the Australian Museum.

Kelsey, Elin. *Strange New Species: Astonishing Discoveries of Life on Earth*. Toronto: Maple Tree Press, 2005.

SQUIDS, OCTOPUSES, AND THEIR RELATIVES

Colossal Squid. **www.squid.tepapa.govt.nz** An interactive online exhibit of Te Papa Museum, New Zealand.

Markle, Sandra. *Outside and Inside Giant Squid*. New York: Walker Books for Young Readers, 2005.

Trueit, Trudi Strain. *Octopuses, Squids, and Cuttlefish*. New York: Franklin Watts, 2002.

SEA SCORPIONS AND SCORPIONS

Bradley, Timothy J. *Paleo Bugs: Survival of the Creepiest*. San Francisco: Chronicle Books, 2008.

Camper, Cathy. *Bugs Before Time: Prehistoric Insects and Their Relatives*. New York: Simon & Schuster Children's Publishing, 2002.

Lassieur, Allison. *Scorpions: The Sneaky Stingers*. New York: Franklin Watts, 2000.

Platypuses

Caper, William. *Platypus: A Century-Long Mystery*. New York: Bearport Publishing, 2008.

Grant, Tom. *Platypus*. 4th ed. Collingwood, Australia: CSIRO Publishing, 2007.

Moyal, Ann. *Platypus: The Extraordinary Story of How a Curious Creature Baffled the World*. Washington, DC: Smithsonian Institution Press, 2001.

Whales

"Whale Origins." **www.neoucom.edu/DEPTS/ANAT/Thewissen/whale_origins** An introduction to the origins of whales on the Thewissen Lab website.

Whales (Investigate Series). North Vancouver, BC: Whitecap Books, 2000.

Wilson, Ben, and Angus Wilson. *Whale-Watchers Handbook*. St. Paul, MN: Voyageur Press, 2006.

Ducks, Geese, and Dromornithids

Miller, Sara Swan. *Waterfowls: From Swans to Screamers*. New York: Franklin Watts, 1999.

Murray, Peter F., and Patricia Vickers-Rich. *Magnificent Mihirungs: The Colossal Flightless Birds of the Australian Dreamtime*. Bloomington and Indianapolis: Indiana University Press, 2004.

"Thunder Birds." *The Family Dromornithidae*. **www.austmus.gov.au/birds/factsheets/thunder_birds.htm** An online fact sheet of the Australian Museum.

Selected Bibliography

Attenborough, David. *Life in the Undergrowth*. Princeton and Oxford: Princeton University Press, 2005.

Attenborough, David. *The Life of Birds*. Princeton, NJ: Princeton University Press, 1998.

The Australian. "Octopuses have Two Legs, Scientists Discover," August 13, 2008.

Braddy, Simon J., Markus Poschmann, and O. Erik Tetlie. "Giant Claw Reveals the Largest Ever Arthropod." *Biology Letters* 4 (2008): 106–109.

Brownell, Philip, and Gary Polis, eds. *Scorpion Biology and Research*. Oxford and New York: Oxford University Press, 2001.

Buchsbaum, Ralph, Mildred Buchsbaum, John Pearse, and Vicki Pearse. *Animals Without Backbones*. 3rd ed. Chicago and London: The University of Chicago Press, 1987.

Byatt, Andrew, Alastair Fothergill, and Martha Holmes. *The Blue Planet: Seas of Life*. New York: DK Publishing, 2001.

Cannings, Richard, Sydney Cannings, and Marja de Jong Westman. *Life in the Pacific Ocean*. Vancouver and Toronto: Greystone Books, 1999.

Carroll, Sean B. *The Making of the Fittest*. New York and London: W.W. Norton & Company, 2006.

Carwardine, Mark, R. Ewan Fordyce, Peter Gill, and Erich Hoyt. *Whales, Dolphins, & Porpoises*. San Francisco: Fog City Press, 1998.

Census of Marine Life. *2007/2008 Highlights Report*, 2008, www.coml.org/pressreleases/highlights08/coml_highlightsReport08-sm.pdf (accessed November 30, 2008).

Clarke, Matt. "New Study Shows Squid Parental Care." *Practical Fishkeeping*, December 16, 2005, www.practicalfishkeeping.co.uk/pfk/pages/item.php?news=791 (accessed December 15, 2008).

Coppold, Murray, and Wayne Powell. *A Geoscience Guide to The Burgess Shale*. Field, BC: The Burgess Shale Geoscience Foundation, 2006.

Cronin, Leonard. *Key Guide to Australian Mammals*. Balgowlah, New South Wales: Reed Books, 1991.

Ellis, Richard. *Aquagenesis: The Origin and Evolution of Life in the Sea*. New York: Viking, 2001.

Grant, Tom. *Platypus*. 4th ed. Collingwood, Australia: CSIRO Publishing, 2007.

Hamilton, Garry. "The Platypus." *Australian Geographic*, October-December 1988, no. 12: 51–67.

Harrison, Richard, and M. M. Bryden. *Whales, Dolphins and Porpoises*. New York and Oxford: Facts On File Publications, 1988.

Hearn, Kelly. "Alien-like Squid with 'Elbows' Filmed at Drilling Site." *National Geographic News*, November 24, 2008, http://news.nationalgeographic.com/news/pf/98196571.html (accessed November 29, 2008).

Hoffman, Jennifer. *Science 101: Ocean Science*. New York: HarperCollins Publishing, 2007.

McLeod, Myles, and Simon Braddy. "Invasion Earth!" *New Scientist*, June 8, 2002.

Moyal, Ann. *Platypus: The Extraordinary Story of How a Curious Creature Baffled the World*. Washington, DC: Smithsonian Institution Press, 2001.

Murray, Peter F., and Patricia Vickers-Rich. *Magnificent Mihirungs: The Colossal Flightless Birds of the Australian Dreamtime*. Bloomington and Indianapolis: Indiana University Press, 2004.

New Scientist. "Bizarre Genetic Makeup of the Platypus Revealed," May 7, 2008.

New York Times. "Colossal Squid has Biggest Eyes in the Animal World, Scientists Say," April 30, 2008.

Norris, Scott. "Platypus Genome Reveals Secrets of Mammal Evolution." *National Geographic News*, May 7, 2008.

Pain, Stephanie. "The Demon Duck of Doom." *New Scientist*, May 27, 2000.

Protheroe, Donald R. *Evolution: What the Fossils Say and Why it Matters*. New York: Columbia University Press, 2007.

Rouse, Greg W., and Fredrik Pleijel. *Polychaetes*. Oxford: Oxford University Press, 2001.

Rowe, Timothy, Thomas H. Rich, Patricia Vickers-Rich, Mark Springer, and Michael O. Woodburne. "The Oldest Platypus and its Bearing on Divergence Timing of the Platypus and Echidna Clades." *PNAS* 105 (January 2008), no. 4: 1238–42.

Spoor, F., S. Bajpal, S. T. Hussain, K. Kumar, and J. G. M. Thewissen. "Vestibular Evidence for the Evolution of Aquatic Behaviour in Early Cetaceans." *Nature* 417 (May 2002): 163–65.

Tetlie, O. Erik. "Distribution and Dispersal History of Eurypterida (Chelicerata)." *Palaeo* 252 (2007): 557–74.

Tetlie, O. Erik, Danita S. Brandt, and Derek E. G. Briggs. "Ecdysis in Sea Scorpions (Chelicerata: Eurypterida)." *Palaeo* 265 (2008): 182–94.

Thewissen, J. G. M., Lisa Noelle Cooper, Mark T. Clementz, Sunil Bajpai, and B. N. Tiwari. "Whales Originated from Aquatic Artiodactyls in the Eocene Epoch of India." *Nature* 27 (December 2007): 1190–95.

Thwaites, Tim. "Duck-billed Platypus had a South American Cousin." *New Scientist*, August 24, 1991.

Walker, Matt. "Cuttlefish Spot Target Prey Early." *BBC News*, June 5, 2008, http://news.bbc.co.uk/2/hi/science/nature/7435757.stm (accessed November 29, 2008).

Ward, Peter D. *Under a Green Sky: Global Warming, the Mass Extinctions of the Past and What They can Tell us About Our Future.* Washington, DC: Smithsonian Books, 2008.

Ward, Peter Douglas. *In Search of Nautilus.* New York: Simon and Schuster, 1988.

Ward, Peter Douglas. *On Methuselah's Trail.* New York: W.H. Freeman and Company, 1992.

Warren, Wesley C., et al. "Genome Analysis of the Platypus Reveals Unique Signatures of Evolution." *Nature* 453 (May 2008): 175–84.

Whyte, Martin A. "A Gigantic Fossil Arthropod Trackway." *Nature* 438 (December 2005): 576.

Wilson, Ben, and Angus Wilson. *Whale-Watchers Handbook.* St. Paul, MN: Voyageur Press, 2006.

Wroe, Stephen. "The Bird From Hell?" *Nature Australia*, Summer 1999–2000: 56–63.

Wroe, Stephen. "Killer Kangaroos and Other Murderous Marsupials." *Scientific American* 280 (May 1999), no. 5. Republished in *Scientific American* Special Edition 14 (March 2004), no. 2: 48–55.

Young, Emma. "Platypus Genome is as Weird as it Looks." *New Scientist News Service*, May 7, 2008.

Zimmer, Carl. *At the Water's Edge: Fish with Fingers, Whales with Legs, and How Life Came Ashore but Then Went Back to the Sea.* New York: Touchstone, 1998.

95

PHOTO CREDITS

ACKNOWLEDGMENTS

My thanks to the following people who provided information, checked facts, explained mysteries, and kept me up to date on the latest research in rapidly changing areas of science:

- Greg Rouse of the Scripps Institution of Oceanography in California, for his expert help with polychaetes and their world;
- Ron O'Dor, Senior Scientist with the Census of Marine Life, for keeping me straight on cephalopods;
- Simon J. Braddy and David Legg of the University of Bristol, for their endless patience in explaining eurypterid and scorpion family ties;
- Jenny Graves of the Australian National University, a member of the team that mapped the platypus genome, for helping me understand that strangest of mammals;
- Hans Thewissen of the Thewissen Lab at Northeastern Ohio Universities, for his knowledge of the evolution of whales;
- Walter Boles of the Australian Museum, for his invaluable help in sorting out the dromornithids.

Any errors in this book are mine, not theirs.

ABOUT THE AUTHOR

CLAIRE EAMER is a full-time writer who loves books, animals, gadgets, travel, and asking questions. Writing about science lets her ask as many questions as she wants— so she likes to write about science. She especially likes writing about science for kids because they have at least as many questions as she has.

BY THE SAME AUTHOR
SUPER CROCS & MONSTER WINGS: MODERN ANIMALS' ANCIENT PAST

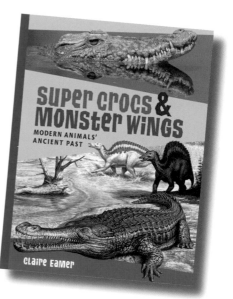

It's hard to imagine, but about 99 percent of all the species that ever lived are already extinct. But some animals didn't vanish altogether, and their distant relatives live among us today.

Author Claire Eamer distills millions of years of global history on the astonishing evolution of six modern-day animals, while artists' renderings bring the ancient creatures to life.

"Without compromising clarity or accuracy, this book provides a 'wow' scientific experience."—*School Library Journal*

100